TRAVEL WITH THE GREAT EXPLORERS

Explore with

Sieur de La Salle

Cynthia O'Brien

Crabtree Publishing Company
www.crabtreebooks.com

Crabtree Publishing Company
www.crabtreebooks.com

Author: Cynthia O'Brien
**Publishing plan research
and development:** Reagan Miller
Managing editor: Tim Cooke
Editor: Shannon Welbourn
Proofreader: Wendy Scavuzzo
Designer: Lynne Lennon
Picture manager: Sophie Mortimer
Design manager: Keith Davis
Editorial director: Lindsey Lowe
Children's publisher: Anne O'Daly
**Production coordinator
and prepress technician:** Tammy McGarr
Print coordinator: Katherine Berti

Produced by Brown Bear Books for
Crabtree Publishing Company

Photographs:
Front Cover: Shutterstock: Jody Ann br; Thinkstock: istockphoto tr,
cr; Topfoto: The Granger Collection main.

Interior: Archives Nationales de France: 16; Archives of Ontario:
12-13; Art Archive: 21t; Bridgeman Art Library: 11t;
Library of Congress: 18, 19b; National Archaeological Museum of
Spain: 14; National Archives of Canada: 5t; Public Domain: 7t,
Alexandrew de Batz 21b; Robert Hunt Library: 13, 14-15, 19t, 24;
Shutterstock: 15br. 17b, 26t, Mark Baldwin 26, Sergio Boccardo 23b,
Jody Dingle 7b, Erick Margarita Images 25b, Jose Fauer 25t,
J. Gorzynik 11b, Tom Gundy 24t, Amy Johansson 27b, Katalin
Kiszaly 23t, Brian Lasenby 22, Nagel Photography 29b, Nicku 12t,
Hein Nouwens 10, Peresanz 4t, SF Photo 29t; Thinkstock: Hemera 5b,
istockphoto 6, 28; Topfoto: The Granger Collection 4b, 17t, 20, 27t.

All other artwork and maps © Brown Bear Books Ltd.

Library and Archives Canada Cataloguing in Publication

O'Brien, Cynthia (Cynthia J.), author
    Explore with Sieur de La Salle / Cynthia O'Brien.

(Travel with the great explorers)
Includes index.
Issued in print and electronic formats.
ISBN 978-0-7787-1430-9 (bound).--ISBN 978-0-7787-1436-1 (pbk.).--
ISBN 978-1-4271-7595-3 (pdf).--ISBN 978-1-4271-7581-6 (html)

    1. La Salle, Robert Cavelier, sieur de, 1643-1687--Juvenile
literature. 2. Explorers--Mississippi River Valley--Biography--
Juvenile literature. 3. Explorers--France--Biography--Juvenile
literature. 4. Mississippi River Valley--Discovery and exploration--
French--Juvenile literature. 5. Canada--History--To 1763 (New
France)--Juvenile literature. 6. Canada--Discovery and exploration--
French--Juvenile literature. I. Title.

FC362.1.L37O63 2014   j971.01'63092   C2014-903664-7
                                            C2014-903665-5

Library of Congress Cataloging-in-Publication Data

O'Brien, Cynthia (Cynthia J.)
 Explore with Sieur de la Salle / Cynthia O'Brien.
    pages cm. -- (Travel with the great explorers)
 Includes index.
 ISBN 978-0-7787-1430-9 (reinforced library binding) --
 ISBN 978-0-7787-1436-1 (pbk.) --
 ISBN 978-1-4271-7595-3 (electronic pdf) --
 ISBN 978-1-4271-7581-6 (electronic html)
    1. La Salle, Robert Cavelier, sieur de, 1643-1687--Juvenile literature.
 2. Explorers--North America--Biography--Juvenile literature. 3.
Explorers--France--Biography--Juvenile literature. 4. Canada--
History--To 1763 (New France)--Juvenile literature. 5. Mississippi
River--Discovery and exploration--French--Juvenile literature. I. Title.

 F1030.5.O37 2015
 910.92--dc23
 [B]
                                            2014020433

Crabtree Publishing Company

www.crabtreebooks.com   1-800-387-7650

Printed in Hong Kong/082014/BK20140613

Published in Canada
Crabtree Publishing
616 Welland Ave.
St. Catharines, ON
L2M 5V6

Published in the United States
Crabtree Publishing
PMB 59051
350 Fifth Avenue, 59th Floor
New York, New York 10118

Published in the United Kingdom
Crabtree Publishing
Maritime House
Basin Road North, Hove
BN41 1WR

Published in Australia
Crabtree Publishing
3 Charles Street
Coburg North
VIC, 3058

CONTENTS

Meet the Boss

René-Robert Cavelier, Sieur de La Salle, was a great explorer of the Great Lakes and the Mississippi River. La Salle was admired by many, but hated by others.

TO CHINA

La Salle originally wanted to go to China rather than Canada. The idea of reaching China through Canada stayed in his mind.

THE YOUNG JESUIT

+ La Salle trains at seminary

La Salle trained at the **Jesuit seminary** in Paris and took his **vows**. The Catholic Church sent many **missionaries** to spread Catholicism in Asia and the **New World**. La Salle asked to go to Asia, but his teachers refused to let him go, so he left the seminary in 1667 for a new life.

CALL ME SIEUR

☛ Second son for Cavelier family

☛ The La Salle estate

La Salle was born on November 21, 1643, in Rouen, France. He was the second son of Jean Cavelier, a merchant, and Catherine Geest. The family owned a large estate called La Salle. During the 1600s, it was common to call sons by the estate name. René-Robert took the title "Sieur de La Salle," meaning "Sir of La Salle."

ADVENTURE AWAITS

★ **La Salle sails to New France**

★ **Landowner in the New World**

La Salle decided to set sail for the New World. His older brother was already a priest in New France, in what is now Canada. He belonged to an order called the Sulpicians. La Salle arrived in Montreal in November 1667. Immediately, his brother granted him land owned by the Sulpicians. La Salle spent the next two years in New France as a **seigneur**, or landowner.

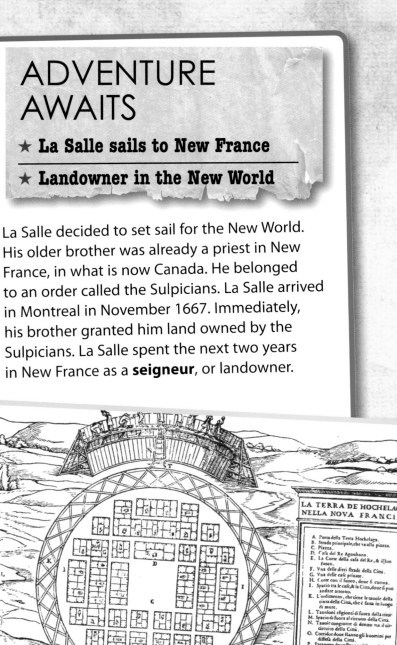

LA TERRA DE HOCHELAGA NELLA NOVA FRANCIA

A. Porta della Terra Hochelaga.
B. Strada principale, che va alla piazza.
C. Piazza.
D. Casa del Re Agouhana.
E. La Corte della casa del Re, & il suo fuoco.
F. Vna delle dieci strade della Città.
G. Vna delle case priuate.
H. Corte con il fuoco, doue si cucina.
I. Spacio tra le case, & la Città,doue si puo andare attorno.
K. L'ordimento, che tiene le tauole della cinta della Città, che è fatta in luogo di mure.
L. Tauoloni c6gionti di fuora della città.
M. Spacio di fuora al circuito della Città.
N. Tauole congionte di dentro vra il circuito della Città.
O. Corridor doue stanno gli huomini per difesa della Città.
P. Parapetto doue stanno gli huomini alla difesa.
Q. Il vacuo che è tra vna tauola, e l'altra, doue è l'ordimento che tien le tauole.
R. Indiani, & Indiane,& putti che sono di fuori della Città p vedere li Francesi.
S. Francesi che entrano nella Città, & che toccano la mano alli Indiani,che erano di fuori della Città appresso al fuoco,& si fanno carezze.
T. La Scala che va su'l Corridor.

Did you know?

Monks and priests sailed on many expeditions. In New France, the Sulpicians tried to convert native peoples to Christianity. The monks built settlements and farmed.

My Explorer Journal

★ **Sieur de La Salle asked the priests who were educating him to send him to China as a missionary. Write a letter from La Salle explaining the qualities he believes a good missionary should have.**

A LIAR AND A CHEAT!

+ King deceived!

In 1684, La Salle asked King Louis XIV to fund an expedition to the Mississippi **Delta**, which he had sailed down two years before. To make his case, La Salle had false maps drawn to show the king. The maps showed the Mississippi close to New Spain (now Mexico). In fact, it was over 400 miles (644 km) away. The king did not want to spend money on exploring. But when La Salle told him it would be possible to strike a blow at the Spanish, the king agreed.

Where Are We Heading?

La Salle's travels took him from New France to the Gulf of Mexico. La Salle claimed a vast land for France—but failed to find it again on his return voyage.

EARLY YEARS

★ **Sulpicians grant land to new arrival**

La Salle built a fort, Saint Sulpice, in what is now Montreal. He still wanted to visit China—his estate was even nicknamed "La Chine," French for "China." La Salle explored New France. He said he learned the Iroquoian language during this time.

GO WEST!

☛ **Heading downriver**

☛ **Crew splits up**

In July 1669, La Salle led an expedition of missionaries down the St. Lawrence River into Lake Ontario. After meeting with local Senecas, the expedition headed to Burlington Bay, on Lake Ontario. La Salle fell ill and went back to Montreal, while the missionaries continued west. Later, La Salle claimed he had found the Ohio River, but historians doubt that his claim is true.

THE GREAT LAKES

★ **Explorer finds inland seas**

★ **Builds forts for France**

About ten years after his first journey, La Salle explored the Great Lakes again. He sailed through Lake Erie and Lake Huron. He then headed south through Lake Michigan and continued by canoe to the St. Joseph River, where he built Fort Miami. At the Illinois River, he built Fort Crèvecoeur. In early 1680, La Salle returned to New France for supplies.

IN THE NAME OF THE KING

☛ **The mighty Mississippi**

La Salle returned to Illinois in late 1681 and set out down the Mississippi River. Using Native American guides, La Salle and his lieutenant, Henri de Tonti, explored until they reached the mouth of the river. On April 9, 1682, La Salle claimed the land for France. He named it Louisiana after King Louis XIV of France.

FATEFUL JOURNEY

+ **A failed colony**

Back in France, La Salle wanted to return to Louisiana. He convinced King Louis XIV to let him go back. In July 1684, La Salle sailed for the Gulf of Mexico with four ships. One ship was lost to pirates; another ran aground. A third headed back to France with many colonists. La Salle built a fort for the colonists who were still stranded in America. He searched for the Mississippi Delta, but never found it again.

La Salle's Exploration of North America

La Salle made two journeys through North America from New France. On the second journey, he reached the Gulf of Mexico. He returned there by sea from France and landed in what is now Texas.

Fort St. Louis
On La Salle's way back up the Mississippi River from his first journey to Louisiana, he founded this fort.

NORTH AMERICA

Fort St. Louis

Fort Crèvecoeur

Louisiana
La Salle and Henri de Tonti believed that Louisiana was a perfect settlement site. Although La Salle had found it while exploring south from Canada in 1682, he failed to find it again in 1685 when he crossed the Atlantic Ocean from France.

Louisiana

Texas
In 1685, La Salle and 180 French colonists arrived near Matagorda Bay and set up Fort St. Louis. La Salle searched for the mouth of the Mississippi River, but the colonists grew frustrated with his leadership. In March 1687, his own men ambushed and killed him.

Fort St. Louis

Gulf of Mexico

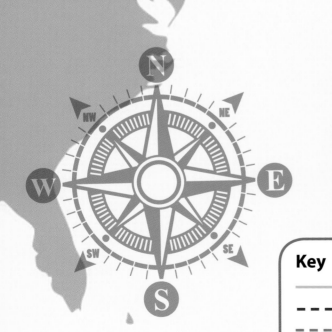

Fort Frontenac

The French built this fort at the mouth of the Cataraqui River to control the fur trade on the Great Lakes. La Salle took control of it in 1675 and strengthened its defenses with limestone walls and **bastions**.

Montreal

La Salle's seigneurie at St. Sulpice was located in the heart of the French government in New France. This area is now known as the suburbs of Montreal.

Ohio River

La Salle claimed to have sailed down the Ohio River in 1669. He hoped that it would offer a shortcut to China, but he was disappointed.

Fort Crèvecoeur

La Salle founded this fort on the Mississippi River in 1680. He named it "broken heart" because it was built in difficult conditions, with harsh winter weather and the desertion of some of his men.

NEW FRANCE

Fort Frontenac

Montreal

Locator map

Key

→ **Possible journey, 1669**

- - → **La Salle's journey, 1682**

- - → **Final journey, 1685–1687**

Meet the Crew

La Salle's travels depended greatly on the support of rich men and powerful friends in France who aided his ambitions to explore in New France. Despite his supporters, he also made bitter enemies.

ROYAL DOUBTER

- ☛ **Explorer seeks king's approval**
- ☛ **Spanish rivalry spurs the king**

La Salle's **ally**, Louis de Buade, Comte de Frontenac, asked King Louis XIV to help La Salle in his early years. However, when La Salle claimed Louisiana, the king was not impressed and said, "I am convinced … that the discovery of Sieur de La Salle is quite useless." The king changed his mind and allowed La Salle to return to the Mississippi to establish a **colony** there.

LIKE MINDS

- ★ **La Salle befriends Comte de Frontenac**

In 1672, the Comte de Frontenac became **governor** of New France. Frontenac, like La Salle, was eager to expand French territory. The comte urged La Salle to build forts and explore. However, Frontenac upset the Iroquois and lost the support of the king. He lost his post in 1682, but returned as governor in 1689.

ON THE RIVER

+ Loyal friend

La Salle's lieutenant, Henri de Tonti, helped to explore the Mississippi River. When La Salle returned to France, Tonti explored on his own voyage to Louisiana. In 1693, six years after La Salle's death, Tonti wrote about his travels with La Salle. In the early 1700s, Tonti was helpful in bringing the Choctaw and Chickasaw people peacefully together after a period of war.

PRIEST AND SCRIBE

+ Journals describe great falls

Louis Hennepin was a Franciscan missionary and writer. He joined La Salle on his expedition through the Great Lakes. Hennepin's writings were the first to describe Niagara Falls. He called it "the most beautiful and altogether the most terrifying waterfall in the universe."

OBJECTION!

☛ New governor blocks La Salle

☛ King displeased

King Louis XIV appointed a new governor for New France in 1682. Joseph-Antoine La Fèbvre de la Barre replaced La Salle's ally, Frontenac. La Barre disliked La Salle. He seized La Salle's forts and blocked further exploration or trade. La Barre stirred up trouble with the Iroquois and caused violent conflicts. Meanwhile, La Salle regained favor with Louis XIV. After just three years, La Barre left Montreal and retired to France.

Check Out the Ride

On his long travels, La Salle walked, canoed, or traveled by ship. On his voyage to the Gulf of Mexico in 1865, he lost one ship to pirates. Two more ran aground.

CANOE

Native peoples showed the French how to make canoes. Birch bark was shaped over a wooden frame. Canoes were light but strong, and could travel in shallow waters.

TRAVEL UPDATE

Canoes ideal for river journey

★ Birch bark canoes were light and narrow. They were ideal for river exploration. For his first expedition, La Salle bought nine canoes and loaded them with food, guns, and blankets. Then he set off down the St. Lawrence River.

THE GRIFFON

☛ First ship to sail the Great Lakes

☛ La Salle builds barque

At Cayuga Creek, La Salle asked Henri de Tonti to build a ship for traveling on the Great Lakes. De Tonti built the *Griffon*, a 59-foot-long (18-m) **barque** with five cannons. It had plenty of space to carry goods. The *Griffon* took La Salle and his men as far as Green Bay, Michigan. Then, they continued their journey in canoes.

OCEAN VESSELS

+ Naval ships for Mississippi expedition

When King Louis XIV gave La Salle permission to sail to the Gulf of Mexico, he ordered the French navy to provide two ships. The 34-gun **man-of-war**, *Le Joly*, carried the colonists. It was accompanied by the barque, *La Belle*, which carried six guns. La Salle hired two more ships to carry supplies for the new colony. He leased a **frigate**, *l'Aimable,* and a **ketch**, *Saint-François*. Only *Le Joly* survived to return to France.

Did you know?

The *Griffon* disappeared and was presumed sunk or captured. In 2004, a wreck believed to be the *Griffon* was discovered in Lake Michigan.

UNCOVERING HISTORY

★ **Belle discovered after 310 years**

★ **Ship preserved in the mud**

In 1995, archaeologists uncovered La Salle's lost ship, *La Belle*. It sank in Matagorda Bay, where mud kept the air away from most of the ship's contents. This helped preserve the over one million **artifacts** that were recovered, including tools, muskets, dishes, ropes, and more.

Solve It with Science

Although La Salle was a leader and an explorer, he was not a sailor, navigator, or mapmaker. When he tried to return to the Mississippi River, he failed to find it.

TOOLS OF THE TRADE

- Equipment onboard
- La Salle lacks key ability

Explorers in the 17th century navigated using a **compass** to find their way. Sailors also used an **astrolabe**. It measured the height of the sun or stars to find how far north or south they were. By the mid-1600s, explorers also used mathematical tables to navigate. Although La Salle used these tools, he was not a skilled navigator. Members of his crew helped him.

TRAVEL UPDATE

A path to China?

★ The explorer La Salle learned from the Seneca about a river they called "Ohio," which means "beautiful." He said the river led to the Pacific Ocean—and from there to China. But La Salle had not found this river, so his story was a little unlikely.

MAPS AND CHARTS

★ **Is that map the right way up?**

★ **Explorer doesn't know where he is**

By the mid-1600s, French explorers, such as Samuel de Champlain and Jesuit missionaries, had helped to map parts of New France. But La Salle was not a **cartographer**. On his first expedition, he took along Abbé René de Bréhan de Galinée so they could draw maps of their explorations. Galinée wrote that La Salle "was undertaking this journey almost in a daze, more or less not knowing where he was going." La Salle's inability to make or use maps led to tragedy on his last journey.

My Explorer Journal

★ **Imagine that you are La Salle. Write a note explaining what you hoped to gain by misleading the king about the location of the Mississippi Delta.**

FIRE

+ Gunpowder startles Native peoples

The French did not allow colonists to trade guns or gunpowder with Native peoples until 1681. The people in Illinois and along the Mississippi were scared of La Salle's guns. La Salle scattered gunpowder around the edge of his camp. If Native peoples came too close, he set fire to it so it ignited. Some Native peoples believed it had magical powers.

Hanging at Home

While La Salle traveled, daily life was often difficult and uncomfortable. Despite his understanding of the conditions, he had little patience for hearing complaints from his companions.

GENTLEMAN FARMER

+ Seigneur La Salle

The French king granted land in New France to nobles and religious orders. These plots of land, where colonists worked, were called *seigneuries*. The owner of the land was called a *seigneur*. La Salle was seigneur of Saint Sulpice, and then of Fort Frontenac. But this comfortable life was of no interest to him. He dreamed of building the fur trade and claiming new territories for France.

AT HOME IN THE FORT

★ **Explorer builds series of forts**

★ **Forts are well-defended trading posts**

In 1675, La Salle was given a trading post by Governor Frontenac, for whom he renamed it Fort Frontenac. La Salle built new stone walls. Southwest of Lake Michigan, La Salle built Fort St. Louis and, farther south, Fort Crèvecoeur.

Did you know?

The first forts were simple structures. They had walls made from upright logs to provide protection. Inside, there were huts for sleeping.

DOOMED

- Basic living conditions
- Colonists sick and hungry

In Texas, La Salle chose a temporary site for a colony. He planned to move once he found the Mississippi. Meanwhile, the colonists built some huts and a two-story building. They had lost many **provisions** when *La Belle* sank. They tried to hunt game and plant crops but were not successful. Many colonists died from disease. Those who survived feared attacks by the Karankawa.

Weather Forecast

ICY CONDITIONS

In March 1680, La Salle was stuck in wintry conditions at Fort Crèvecoeur with few supplies. La Salle and some of his men walked 1,000 miles (1,609 km) to Fort Frontenac. The men cut their way through thick forests and had no shelter at night. It took three months before they reached Fort Frontenac.

Meeting and Greeting

La Salle carefully managed his relationships with the Native people. He used them as guides and made peace where he could. The most feared were the Iroquois, a confederacy of five nations.

NEW NEIGHBORS

★ **Allies and enemies**

★ **Iroquois block trade**

The French wanted to extend their fur trade, but the routes were blocked by the Iroquois. The Iroquois were allied with the English in New York. In 1673, La Salle set up a meeting between Governor Frontenac and the Iroquois, which led to the building of Fort Frontenac. The fort protected trade along Lake Ontario.

THE SENECA

☛ **La Salle approaches Iroquois nation**

☛ **Locals suspicious of French plans**

Near Niagara, La Salle met the Seneca. They were members of the Iroquois Confederacy who lived on Lake Ontario and traded with the English. They did not want La Salle to trade in their territory but, in the end, they let him build his ship.

TENSIONS MOUNT

☞ **Seneca plot against La Salle**

☞ **Armed ship launches**

As La Salle prepared the *Griffon*, the Seneca watched. They plotted to set fire to the ship, but they did not carry out their plan. They were surprised by the ship's appearance. The *Griffon* was so large that it looked to them like a floating fort. When the ship launched, the crew fired its cannons. This frightening sound sent the Seneca running.

At War

The introduction of gunpowder weapons gave the Iroquois an advantage when they waged war against rival Native peoples, such as the Algonquians.

TRADE WARS

+ **Changing partners**

+ **English vs French**

In 1670, the English established the Hudson's Bay Company in New France. This disrupted the French fur trade. The English also had trading posts in what is now New England. The Iroquois used English weapons to raid Huron settlements. Meanwhile, wars among Native peoples to the west made it difficult to trade there. La Salle expanded the French fur trade by giving the Illinois people guns in return for furs. For the first time, the Illinois had firearms to use against European settlers.

Building Relationships

As La Salle traveled south from New France, he encountered new and different cultures. Not all of them were happy to see the French arrive, and some became openly hostile.

MIDDLEMEN

★ Illinois traders

★ New French allies

The Illinois people traded with the Algonquian and Ottawa people to the north, and with the Osage and Missouri people to the south and west. In 1680, La Salle met the Illinois who lived in a village called Pimitoui. This is now Peoria, Illinois. They did not trust La Salle and his friendship with the Iroquois. La Salle convinced the Illinois people that he could protect them if he built a fort.

Did you know?

The Illinois welcomed La Salle with a ceremony. They were eager to trade, once they knew that they could trust the French explorer.

THEFT AND VIOLENCE

+ Coastal people attack

The Karankawa lived along the Texas coast of the Gulf of Mexico. They were semi-**nomadic** people. La Salle arrived at Matagorda Bay in 1685. At first, the Karankawa were peaceful. But after one of La Salle's ships ran aground, he accused them of stealing blankets from the wreck. In turn, the Karankawa accused La Salle of stealing their canoes and killed some of the men. After learning that La Salle was dead, the Karankawa attacked the tiny settlement at Fort St. Louis and killed nearly all of the settlers.

Temples

The French found that the Natchez of Louisiana were skilled builders. They had constructed a tall lodge the French decided was a temple.

TRAVEL UPDATE

Locals are friendly

★ At the mouth of the Arkansas River, La Salle met the Quapaw people. Two Quapaw guides accompanied La Salle as he continued down the Mississippi. The Quapaw then introduced La Salle to the Taensa people. The Taensa welcomed the French and exchanged gifts with them. As the expedition continued, La Salle visited a Natchez village and also met the Choctaw people in Louisiana.

I Love Nature

La Salle discovered many new plants and animals. He did not record any of his findings, but Henri de Tonti wrote of the natural riches that were discovered on their expeditions.

Hunted!

Beaver fur was very valuable in Europe. Although the French king tried to control the trade, many **trappers** worked for themselves in the wilderness.

☁ Weather Forecast

UPS AND DOWNS

Near the Great Lakes, the climate can be very harsh. Henri de Tonti described being stuck in the woods in winter. He lived for days on wild garlic that he dug up from beneath the snow. But farther south, in Louisiana, the French were impressed by how pleasant the climate was.

FUR EVERYWHERE!

+ Beavers plentiful

The beavers lived near rivers, lakes, and wetlands in much of North America. The Native peoples were expert hunters and supplied the French and English with beaver **pelts**. When La Salle's expedition arrived in Illinois, Henri de Tonti noted that "**hides** and furs are to be had there almost for nothing."

MONEY GROWS ON TREES

★ **Tonti gets an idea**

Both La Salle and Tonti believed France could make money in Louisiana. One of Tonti's ideas was to produce and trade silk. He wrote, "they [the Native peoples] might be obliged to make silk … bringing to them from France the eggs of silkworms, for the forests are full of mulberry trees. This would be a valuable trade." The French never developed this plan.

WHERE THE BUFFALO ROAM

+ **Arrival in Louisiana**

+ **First impressions**

Tonti and La Salle found rich land around the Mississippi. They noticed the lush fruit trees, and there were many types of animals for fur and food. Tonti wrote that Louisiana was "the most beautiful country in the world, prairies, woods of mulberry trees, vines, and fruits that we are not acquainted with." The French were disappointed about the animals they found. Tonti wrote "there are but few beavers … but there is a large number of buffaloes, bears, large wolves, stags and hinds."

Did you know?

The buffalo was central to the lives of the Plains Indians. They ate its meat and used its skin for clothing. They even had rituals and dances to worship the buffalo gods.

Fortune Hunting

By the mid 1600s, Spain, England, and France had settlements in North America. Each powerful nation wanted to profit from the riches of the New World, so competition was fierce.

PASSION FOR FUR

- Fur trade takes off
- Traders compete for business

La Salle was unpopular in New France because he competed with French and English merchants in the fur trade. He also competed with the *coureurs de bois*, independent fur trappers. Beaver was the most valuable fur. It was used to make felt. Felt hats were the height of fashion in Europe, so prices and profits were high.

OPPORTUNITY KNOCKS

★ French open interior to trade

With the permission of the king, La Salle established forts around the Great Lakes. They were posts for trading with Native peoples. The French traded goods, such as guns and metal products. In return, they received beaver, deer, and bear furs.

IT'S WAR!

+ Spanish declare war on France

+ New World rivals

France and Spain were old rivals. In 1683, Spain declared war on France just as La Salle was trying to return to the Mississippi River from France. Pirates from both countries attacked ships in the Gulf of Mexico. Henri de Tonti assured the king that, "one single post [fort], established towards the lower part of the river, will be sufficient to protect a territory extending more than 800 leagues from north to south, and still farther from east to west."

SHINY AND SILVER

★ Mines attract French

★ Louis XIV to overthrow Spanish

The Spanish controlled many silver mines in northern Mexico. King Louis XIV wanted riches for France. La Salle convinced the king that the land around the Mississippi was rich, too. The king agreed that a French colony could provide a good base. From there, La Salle said they could attack the Spanish mines and make a fortune for France at the same time.

Did you know?

The French and English governments gave licenses to pirates to attack Spanish ships carrying gold and silver from America to Europe.

This Isn't What It Said in the Brochure

The young René-Robert Cavelier, Sieur de La Salle, dreamed of greatness. However, failure and tragedy marked his achievements and adventures. His own men even tried to poison him.

GRIFFON DISAPPEARS!

+ Shipwreck suspected

In Green Bay, Michigan, La Salle loaded the *Griffon* with valuable furs. La Salle gave orders to six crew members to take the ship back to Niagara. The furs would be payment to his **creditors**. On September 18, 1679, the *Griffon* sailed for Niagara but it never arrived. Some people believed that the crew abandoned the ship and sold the furs, while others thought the Iroquois attacked it. The true story of what happened still remains a mystery today.

MUTINY

- Crew abandons their leader
- La Salle poisoned!

The French were unhappy in Illinois. Several men fled back to New France. One man actually poisoned La Salle. Although he was very ill, a remedy he carried saved his life. When La Salle returned to Montreal for supplies, he left Henri de Tonti in charge. The remaining men set fire to the fort and returned to Fort Frontenac. La Salle later punished them.

My Explorer Journal

★ Imagine you are one of the colonists who plotted against La Salle. Write, using details from the text, a defense of your behavior and explain why you turned on your leader.

MURDER AND MAYHEM

★ La Salle murdered by crew

★ Men claim they had no choice

La Salle was a demanding, selfish leader and many of his men didn't like him. Finally, the crew reached their breaking point. On an expedition to find the Mississippi, the crew ambushed their leader. On March 19, 1687, Pierre Duhaut shot and killed La Salle.

Captive!

The children taken from Fort St. Louis lived with the Karankawa for some years. They were freed by Spanish soldiers and became servants in New Spain.

FORT ST. LOUIS

☛ Colonists under siege

☛ Illness takes its toll

At first, about 70 colonists lived at Fort St. Louis in Texas. By the time of La Salle's death in 1687, only 20 colonists remained. Many had died from smallpox and other diseases. Still others died in attacks by the Karankawa. They waited to be rescued, but help never came. In January 1689, the Karankawa killed all of the colonists except six children, whom they took captive.

End of the Road

La Salle was murdered before he was able to achieve all of his dreams. However, he had gained the fame he wanted. His journeys ensured that he would never be forgotten.

LASTING LEGACY

☛ French colonize the south

☛ Colony fails... for now

The French settlement in Texas lasted only a few years. Most of the colonists died, though Henri Joutel, another of La Salle's lieutenants, fled with a few others to France. The children who were taken captive lived with the Karankawa for years before being taken to New Spain. But the French stayed in Texas for another 70 years. Today, many French descendants still live in Louisiana.

Did you know?

After the English drove the French from Canada in 1763, many French colonists made their way to Louisiana. They came from Acadia in Canada, and were known as Cajuns in Louisiana.

FRIEND STAYS LOYAL

★ Tonti seeks La Salle

Henri de Tonti heard that La Salle was in Texas looking for the Mississippi River. He sailed down the river to meet him. By the time Tonti reached the Gulf of Mexico, La Salle was dead and his colony had been attacked by the Karankawa.

Settlers

After La Salle's exploration, French settlement along the St. Lawrence grew. By 1700, there were 9,000 French settlers in Canada; by 1754, the total was 55,000.

ABANDONED DREAMS

+ Fort Crèvecoeur falls to Iroquois

The end of Fort Crèvecoeur came in September 1680. Iroquois warriors attacked the fort and forced Henri de Tonti to flee. In 1682, creditors took Fort Frontenac when La Salle did not pay them. They did not defend it and the Iroquois attacked. In 1695, after La Salle's death, Governor Frontenac rebuilt the fort. However, the British captured it in 1758 and eventually destroyed it. The remains of a few limestone walls of the original fort can still be seen in Kingston, Ontario.

TRAVEL UPDATE

What's in a name?

★ Many places in Canada and the United States bear La Salle's name. The site of Saint Sulpice is now La Salle, part of the city of Montreal. La Salle, Illinois, developed across the river from Starved Rock. LaSalle, Ontario, lies south of Windsor on the Detroit River. The French settled there in the 1700s.

GLOSSARY

ally A person or country who cooperates with another for a particular purpose

barque A sailing ship with three masts

bastions Towers that project from a fort so that its defenders can fire along the walls

cartographer A person who makes maps

colony A settlement or territory that is under the political control of a different country

compass A device used for navigation with a needle that always points to the north

confederacy A league or alliance, especially between groups of peoples

creditors People to whom someone owes money

delta A fan-shaped area of streams and islands

frigate A lightly armed warship

governor A representative of the British Crown in a colony

hides Animal skins that have been treated to preserve them

Jesuit seminary A Catholic school for training priests

ketch A small, two-masted sailing ship

lieutenant A deputy or right-hand man

lodge A Native American structure, especially one built to host religious rituals

man-of-war A sailing ship heavily armed with cannons for fighting

missionaries People who are sent to promote a religion in another country

New World An early European name for the Americas

nomadic Living a life without a permanent home, and moving around often

pelts The skins of animals with the hair or fur still on them

provisions Supplies

seigneur A French word meaning the owner of a manor or estate

trapper A person who catches wild animals for their fur

vows Promises someone makes when becoming a priest, monk, or nun

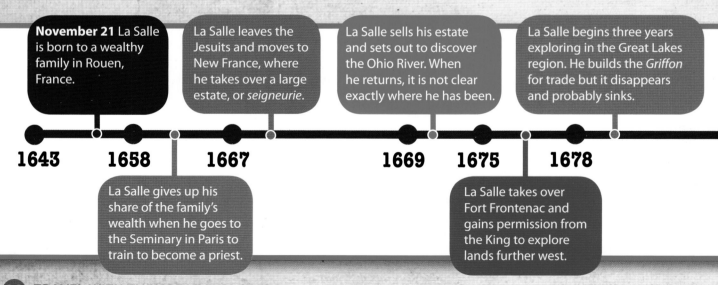

November 21 La Salle is born to a wealthy family in Rouen, France.

La Salle leaves the Jesuits and moves to New France, where he takes over a large estate, or *seigneurie*.

La Salle sells his estate and sets out to discover the Ohio River. When he returns, it is not clear exactly where he has been.

La Salle begins three years exploring in the Great Lakes region. He builds the *Griffon* for trade but it disappears and probably sinks.

1643　**1658**　**1667**　**1669**　**1675**　**1678**

La Salle gives up his share of the family's wealth when he goes to the Seminary in Paris to train to become a priest.

La Salle takes over Fort Frontenac and gains permission from the King to explore lands further west.